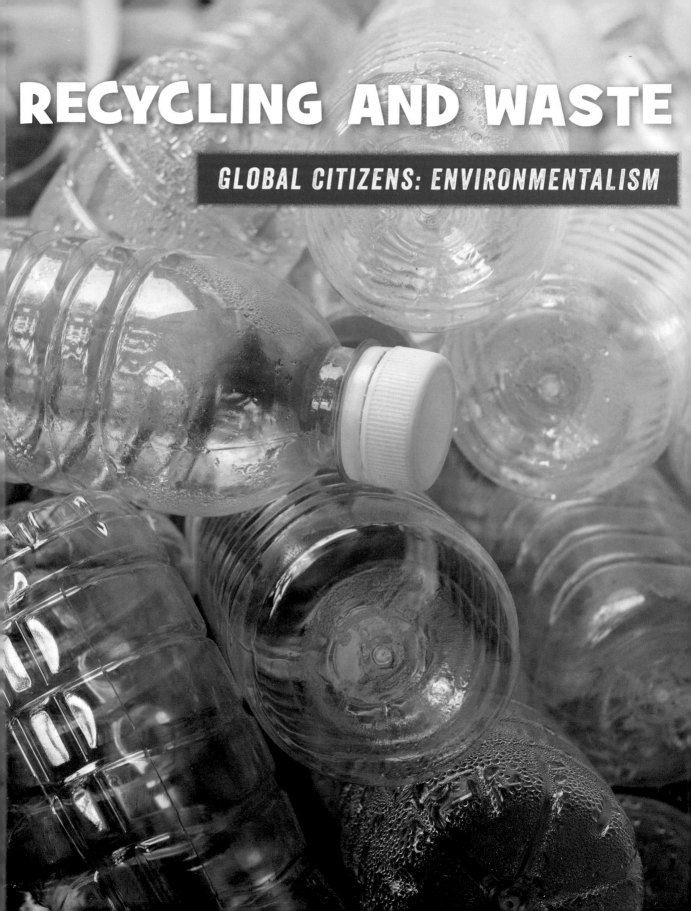

RECYCLING AND WASTE

GLOBAL CITIZENS: ENVIRONMENTALISM

Published in the United States of America by Cherry Lake Publishing
Ann Arbor, Michigan
www.cherrylakepublishing.com

Content Adviser: Michael Rockett MS, Natural resources

Reading Adviser: Marla Conn MS, Ed., Literacy specialist, Read-Ability, Inc.

Photo Credits: © Teerasak Ladnongkhun / Shutterstock.com, cover, 1; © Olexandr Panchenko / Shutterstock.com, 5; © vidguten / Shutterstock.com, 6; © ducu59us / Shutterstock.com, 8; © Supannee_Hickman / Shutterstock.com, 10; © Aerovista Luchtfotografie / Shutterstock.com, 13; © Gabor Havasi / Shutterstock.com, 14; © MeePoohyaPhoto / Shutterstock.com, 16; © Mark Van Scyoc / Shutterstock.com, 19; © KaliAntye / Shutterstock.com, 20; © goory / Shutterstock.com, 22; © Huguette Roe / Shutterstock.com, 25; © tonympix / Shutterstock.com, 26; © suwannee lomklang / Shutterstock.com, 28

Library of Congress Cataloging-in-Publication Data
Names: Labrecque, Ellen, author.
Title: Recycling and waste / Ellen Labrecque.
Description: Ann Arbor : Cherry Lake Publishing, 2017. | Series: Global citizens. Environmentalism |
   Audience: Grades 4 to 6. | Includes bibliographical references and index.
Identifiers: LCCN 2016058620 | ISBN 9781634728713 (hardcover) | ISBN 9781634729604 (pdf) |
   ISBN 9781534100497 (pbk.) | ISBN 9781534101388 (hosted ebook)
Subjects: LCSH: Recycling (Waste, etc.)—Juvenile literature.
Classification: LCC TD794.5 .L33 2017 | DDC 363.72/82—dc23
LC record available at https://lccn.loc.gov/2016058620

Cherry Lake Publishing would like to acknowledge the work of the Partnership for 21st Century Learning.
Please visit *www.p21.org* for more information.

Printed in the United States of America
Corporate Graphics

ABOUT THE AUTHOR

Ellen Labrecque has written over 100 books for children. She is passionate about being a friend to the environment and taking care of our planet. She lives in Pennsylvania with her husband, Jeff, and her two young "editors," Sam and Juliet. She loves running, hiking, and reading.

TABLE OF CONTENTS

CHAPTER 1

History: Making Things New Again 4

CHAPTER 2

Geography: Recycling Around the World 12

CHAPTER 3

Civics: Everybody Helps 18

CHAPTER 4

Economics: The Numbers Behind Recycling 24

THINK ABOUT IT....................................... 30
FOR MORE INFORMATION...............................31
GLOSSARY 32
INDEX... 32

History: Making Things New Again

Environmentalism is a big word. But its meaning is simple. Practicing environmentalism means being a friend to Earth and all its creatures. Environmentalists want to keep our air healthy, our land clean, and our water fresh. They want to take care of our plants and animals by making sure our planet remains a safe place to live. Some environmentalists focus on encouraging people to stop polluting. Others work to protect our plants and animals. One of the most important environmental jobs is to teach people about **recycling**.

The Story of Recycling

Recycling is when something old is broken down and made

Boxes should be flattened before recycling.

Landfills continue to take up more and more space.

into something new. This can be done with paper, plastic, glass, and many metals. The more we recycle, the less trash and waste there is. This means less pollution on our land, in the air, and in our water. By recycling, we also save our **natural resources**, like trees, from being made into new products. For example, 900 million trees are cut down each year to make paper.

The concept of recycling isn't new. In early Roman times, bronze coins were melted down and made into statues. During wartime, the Romans melted down jewelry and made it into weapons. Recycling played an important role during World War II (1939–1945). In the United States, people collected tin cans, scrap metal, and aluminum foil. They also collected old toys and pots and pans. The metals were then melted down and used to make tanks and weapons for fighting in the war.

After the war was over, people didn't recycle as much. Machines and factories created goods cheaply and in mass amounts. People began throwing things out, rather than trying to find a way to reuse or remake them. This new way of life was called "throwaway living." **Landfills** across the country filled up with trash.

The recycling symbol reminds everyone to reduce and reuse.

Earth Day

People began to understand that all this trash was hurting Earth and all its creatures, including humans. They also realized that if this trend continued, we would run out of materials needed to survive. Recycling programs and centers began to pop up across the United States.

In 1964, the all-aluminum can was made. These cans, used for sodas and other drinks, could be recycled to make brand-new cans. Soon afterward, the universal symbol for recycling was created by designer Gary Anderson. There are three arrows forming a triangle. One arrow symbolizes "reduce" (the less things you use, the less waste you have). Another arrow means "reuse" (use things over and over, not just once), and the third one represents recycling.

On April 22, 1970, the first national Earth Day was held. More than 20 million Americans celebrated at fairs throughout the country. The day inspired people to learn about all the ways they can help our planet. They realized recycling is one way to do this.

America generates 243 million tons of trash a year. This is much more than any other country. Today, there are 9,000

Recycling trucks in the United States can come as often
as every week depending on the city.

community curbside recycling programs across the country. We recycle 82 million tons, or about 38 percent of our waste. The goal of the United States is to eventually recycle 75 percent of its total trash.

Developing Questions

Did World War II make Americans better or worse at recycling? What was the purpose of Earth Day?

These two questions are examples of recall questions. Recall questions are meant to help you think about something you just read and answer questions about it. They help you remember and learn from your reading.

CHAPTER 2

Geography: Recycling Around the World

People recycle all over the world. Some countries are better at it than others. Austria and Germany are winning the recycling race. They recycle about 63 percent of their total trash. South Korea isn't far behind: Residents there recycle 59 percent of their garbage.

Ways of the World

Different countries have different ways of encouraging people to recycle. In Germany, the government charges you money for every garbage can you fill up. But recycling is always free. Sweden has converted its garbage into energy. Its burnt-up waste powers about 250,000 homes. However, Sweden has become so good at this, it has run out of garbage! The country takes in trash from its

This is a waste and recycling factory in the Netherlands.

Compost soil is good for plants.

neighbor Norway to keep the power going. Some cities in Canada even recycle cigarette butts. These pieces of litter can be turned into plastic through recycling methods.

Composting

Wasting food is a big problem all over the world. Roughly one-third of the food on Earth, about 1.3 billion tons, gets thrown out. When food waste is dumped into landfills, it releases **methane**, which pollutes the air.

Composting is a word for food recycling. This is when food and plants are put together to **decay** naturally. Instead of food

Gathering and Evaluating Sources

Sometimes it is tough to figure out what can and can't be recycled. It can also be tricky to figure out where to take things to be recycled. Check out www.earth911.com to help you. If you type in your zip code, it tells you the recycling places closest to you.

Different trash cans encourage people to recycle.

wasting away in garbage piles, the compost gets turned into soil to help other plants and crops grow.

One way some countries encourage composting is by having public cans for different purposes. This means people separate their trash. Paper goes in one bin, glass goes in another, and food waste goes in yet another bin. Austria turns 34 percent of its waste into **fertilizer**. This is more than any other country.

San Francisco, California, is trying to become a "zero waste city" by 2020. This means the entire city would send no garbage at all to landfills. San Francisco is already the United States' best city at composting. It sends more than 600 tons of food waste and yard clippings to a facility where it is turned into natural fertilizer! Farms in the area then buy this soil to grow their new plants.

Do You Hear the Music?

People are rewarded with music every time they recycle in Helsingborg, Sweden. The town has installed speakers in its recycling bins. Every time somebody puts a bottle in the bin, a tune is played. It's music to Earth's ears! How might this encourage more people to recycle?

CHAPTER 3

Civics: Everybody Helps

The Environmental Protection Agency (EPA) was started in the United States in 1970. Its goal is to create a cleaner and healthier environment for the American people. One of the ways the EPA tries to do this is through recycling. On its Web site, the EPA teaches people about the importance of recycling. The United States doesn't have any national laws that require people to recycle. Instead, recycling laws differ from state to state.

State-by-State Rules

Some states have stricter laws than others when it comes to recycling. Some states, like Wisconsin and Minnesota, ban

This is the EPA headquarters in Washington, D.C.

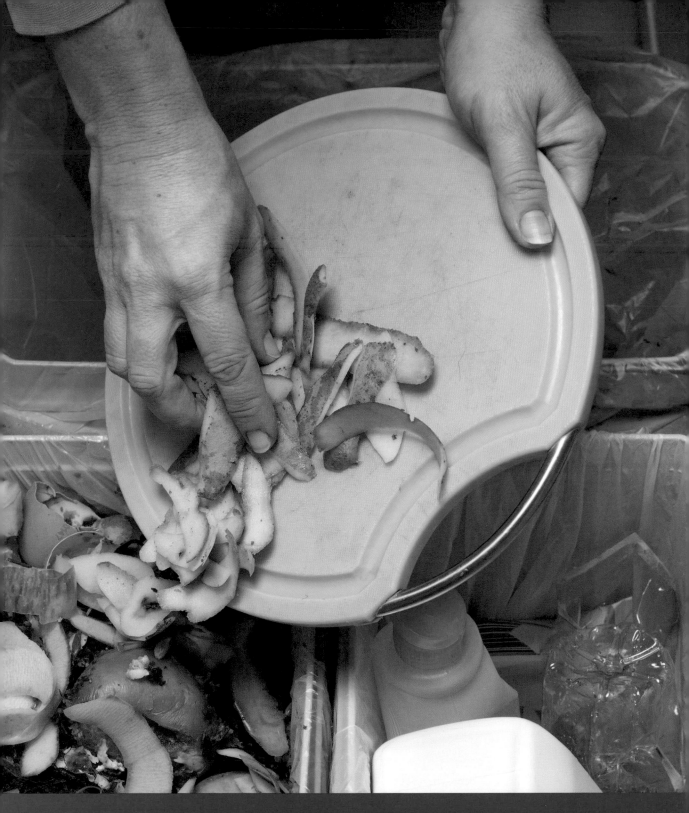

This person is properly separating the compost from the recycling bin.

landfills. Other states, like California and Connecticut, have created "bottle bills." The state pays a certain amount for each bottle or can that a person recycles.

Rhode Island and New Jersey are the best states at recycling. They have more recycling curbside pickups for people, as well as more recycling plants than any of the other states **per capita**. This is partially because they have to: These two small states have the least amount of land for landfills!

Recycling Champions

Since there are no federal laws for recycling, many people and private organizations work to make recycling a top priority.

Recycle Across America is an organization started by businesswoman Michelle Hedlund. The company teaches people the right way to recycle. Many people put garbage into recycling bins. This contaminates, or ruins, everything in the bin, and then nothing in there can be recycled at all. Recycle Across America thinks that if all bins were labeled correctly, this wouldn't happen. They want to ensure every garbage bin is properly labeled for paper, glass, cans and plastic, compost, and landfill.

The steel in cars are made with about 25 percent recycled steel.

All this labeling would cut down on confusion and make recycling easier for everybody.

The Most Recycled Product: Cars

Cars are the most recycled product in the world. Ten million cars a year are recycled in the United States. Recycling all these car parts keeps 11 million tons of steel and other metals out of landfills.

Developing Claims and Using Evidence

Most people think recycling is a good idea. But the United States doesn't have any national laws that require people to recycle. Do some research using the Internet and your local library. Can you find evidence supporting a national law for recycling? Using evidence, form your own opinion on this subject.

CHAPTER 4

Economics: The Numbers Behind Recycling

Recycling doesn't just help the planet; it also generates money and jobs. In the United States, there are more than 50,000 recycling companies with more than one million employees. The payroll for all these people is more than $37 billion a year. The more we recycle, the more jobs and money we bring into our country. This is true around the world, too.

China leads the world in making electronic devices such as cell phones and computers. Many of the products they use to make these devices come from recycled material such as copper. The wires used to charge your cell phones could be from the same copper used to make your Christmas tree lights years ago!

Copper can be recycled an infinite number of times.

There are proper ways of recycling electronics.

Electronic Waste

One of the biggest growing sections of the recycling industry is electronic waste, or e-waste. E-waste is materials from electronic equipment such as computers, cell phones, and tablets. Around the world, 30 million to 50 million tons of electronic equipment is tossed into landfills every year. These devices contain valuable metals such as gold, copper, and silver. The value of all this waste is estimated at $218 billion. Many companies are

Communicating Conclusions

Before reading this book, did you know about recycling? Now that you know more, why do you think this is an important issue? Learn even more about recycling and the importance of helping protect Earth and all its creatures. Every week, look up different organizations that support recycling. Share what you learn with friends at school or with family at home.

Recycling helps us be less wasteful.

working to figure out how best to recycle these electronics. Some companies are starting buy-back programs. They will buy back people's old cell phones and computers and then take them to plants where they can be recycled. This keeps these devices out of landfills and also helps people and companies make money!

Taking Informed Action

Do you want to recycle more but don't know how? There are many ways you can get involved and many different organizations that you can explore. Check them out online. Here are three to help you start your search:

* Recycle Across America: Learn about how this organization works to get labels on all recycling cans across the country.
* Planet Aid: Discover how this organization helps people recycle their clothes and shoes.
* America Recycles Day: Find out about National Recycling Day.

Think About It

Recycling reduces trash in our landfills, stops wild animals from eating garbage they find, and keeps us from cutting down trees and polluting our waters. People around the world recycle. But we can still do so much more. More than 60 percent of the trash in the United States still gets dumped into landfills. How do you think this recycling problem compares to the world's other problems? Use the data you find in your research to support your argument.

For More Information

FURTHER READING

Hall, Eleanor J. *Recycling.* Farmington Hills, MI: KidHaven Press, 2005.

Inskipp, Carol. *Reducing and Recycling Waste.* Milwaukee, WI: Gareth Stevens Publishing, 2005.

Ward, D. J. *What Happens to Our Trash?* New York: HarperCollins Publishers, 2012.

WEB SITES

Earth Day Network
www.earthday.org
Find out more about Earth Day.

Environmental Protection Agency
www3.epa.gov
This is a great place to begin your recycling research.

The Imagination Factory
www.kid-at-art.com
Learn about how you can recycle through art.

GLOSSARY

composting (KAHM-pohst-ing) mixing dying matter in a way that it can be used to help plants grow

decay (dih-KAY) to rot or break down

environmentalism (en-vye-ruhn-MEN-tuhl-iz-uhm) working to protect the air, water, animals, and plants from pollution and other harmful things

fertilizer (FUR-tuh-lize-ur) a substance, whether natural or chemical, that enriches the soil and helps plants grow

landfills (LAND-filz) large outdoor areas used to dump garbage

methane (METH-ane) a gas that can be burned and used for fuel, but can be bad for the environment

natural resources (NACH-ur-uhl REE-sors-iz) things that can be used from nature, such as land, forests, minerals, and water

per capita (PUR KAP-i-tuh) by or for each person in a population

recycling (ree-SYE-kling) breaking something down to make something new from it

INDEX

aluminum, 7, 9
Austria, 12, 16

"bottle bills," 21

Canada, 15
cars, 22, 23
China, 24
composting, 14, 15–16, 17
copper, 24, 25, 27

Earth Day, 9
electronics (e-waste), 27, 29
energy, 12
environmentalism, 4

EPA (Environmental Protection Agency), 18, 19

fertilizer, 16, 17
food waste, 15–16, 17

garbage. *See* trash
Germany, 12

landfills, 6, 7, 15, 17, 21, 23, 27, 29

methane, 15

natural resources, 7
Netherlands, 13

pollution, 7

Recycle Across America, 21, 29
recycling
   around the world, 12–17, 24
   curbside program, 11, 21
   economics of, 24–29
   history, 7
   how to get started, 29
   and jobs, 24
   rules, 18–19
   universal symbol, 8, 9
   what it is, 4–11

San Francisco, 16–17
South Korea, 12
Sweden, 12

"throwaway living," 7
trash, 7, 9
   conversion into energy, 12, 15
   separating, 20, 21

World War II, 7

yard waste, 17

"zero waste city," 16